Hand Signs from Eternity's Yurt

Hand Signs from Eternity's Yurt

Poems by

Diane Raptosh

© 2022 Diane Raptosh. All rights reserved.
This material may not be reproduced in any form, published,
reprinted, recorded, performed, broadcast,
rewritten or redistributed without
the explicit permission of Diane Raptosh.
All such actions are strictly prohibited by law.

Cover design by Shay Culligan
Cover art by Eric Raptosh

ISBN: 978-1-63980-131-2

Kelsay Books
502 South 1040 East, A-119
American Fork, Utah 84003
Kelsaybooks.com

*This book is dedicated to the memory of
Mary Midgley (1919–2018),
to my daughters, Keats and Colette, and to my grandchildren,
Camas and Weston.*

Acknowledgments

Thanks to the editors of the following journals and anthologies in which these poems first appeared, sometimes in earlier versions:

Sonnet II: *New York Times,* 11.26.2020
Sonnets I–X: *Notes from a Biscuit Tin,* poems dedicated to themes of philosopher Mary Midgley
Sonnet XIII: *Rupture: Writers in the Attic* (The Cabin Anthology), 2021

Thanks also to Greg McElwain for introducing me to the British moral philosopher Mary Midgley and inviting me to compose poems in response to her soulful and wide-ranging work, which shows how philosophy can be practically applied to engage the world and transform it. What a thrill it has been to respond to how Midgley explored human nature and the self, connections with animals and the natural world, as well as complexities of morality, gender, science, and more. Composing poems in dialogue with some of her quotations—ranging from the profound to the quotidian—was a great challenge, a joy beyond measure. Here's hoping for continued dialogues between poetry and philosophy.

Contents

Hand Signs from Eternity's Yurt

I.	13
II.	14
III.	15
IV.	16
V.	17
VI.	18
VII.	19
VIII.	20
IX.	21
X.	22
XI.	23
XII.	24
XIII.	25
XIV.	26
XV.	27
XVI.	28
XVII.	29
XVIII.	30
XIX.	31
XX.	32
XXI.	33
[The Floating Sonnet, Unnumbered]	34

Hand Signs from Eternity's Yurt

I.

> *Freedom's meaning is only clear when we specify just what we want to be free from and free for.*
> —Mary Midgley

I prize what praise phrases, and I could keep
riffing all night on the fourteen-spotted
ladybug buried in love's hush-hush mission
of dishing up flavonoids. Then there are days,
out of hope, I devote to harassing capitalism—
its barefaced abortions of so many creatures'
destinies. My brain says to bug. But to sing
is to stash in a phonic grow house this spliff
of deep sea. This stride of trombones. It is
to be what one is in the most slowly debuted
state of risk. To sit still on purpose is no doubt
the birth of defiance's footwork—the one great
too-muchness translating her mind into yours
for the ungodly price of a flick of your Zippo.

II.

Leaves relate not only to other leaves, but to fruit, twigs, branches and the whole tree.
—Mary Midgley

I have this idea the vowels within *Idaho* know
to slipper us into some new, non-tribal unities.
This syncs with a view of the mood of the line
as mode of communion. Which tends to fly in
the worried face of the clank in the world. This
probably suggests it's our due to vacate clans.
Doing so, maybe we'll cruise on past the moving
rockface of meanness. In so many verbs the work
insists we *preserve reality access for all*—
the full while we keep letting nerd gods execute
prog. Which acts will more or less force us to slim
to the singular plural pronouns *we|us|our*—to heap
upon thief and monk. Kestrel. Owl. On Boise's
Bees Knees Saloon and Hamwich Snack Bar.

III.

The self's wholeness, then, is not that of a billiard ball, but that of an organism.
—Mary Midgley

Since I've been furloughed from social routine,

this goddess kites in and squats on the raft

of my tongue. She'll maybe soothe a few spit-dolls,

spin a slow tune from the sixties. Nip some

red plonk. She pretty much taught me how

to just sit in a room with the earthly intelligence—

that old horse eye, that legged piano. The gaze

of rain water, the elms' benediction. Listen.

Why did the bargain insist I must scatter whole

lung-spans of days to life's outer circumference?

My sixth decade of hours makes me feel as I figure

I did when I was not yet. Forgive if I meld

such full-on silence with god—this song

its own means of petting the mind of a dog.

IV.

> *Understanding a habit is seeing what company it keeps.*
> —Mary Midgley

I keep drinking up ways to make power zones
fear me. I name each day *Che,* and my line
of brindled defiance *Extreme Thomas Merton.*
Because we trade in one another's braveries.
Because the bowed world spins out in rhythms.
Because I have made of my ratty throw pillows
itemized hitmen. Because I've been made to
christen the monk in each person a peer outlaw.
Because who doesn't tithe to the nighttime's
four stentorian oarsmen? Because vowels sip
blood just for the *o*'s in it. Because please just
put your cell phone into contemplative mode.

Because *couplet* is *coup,* the sonnet monastic.

Please meet my new saffron dress, Malcom X.

V.

To be free, you have to have an original constitution.
—Mary Midgley

Writing a sonnet leaves the smell of alphabet

on the palms: this plane of fleck-tones, these

prows of clouds hewn in a word in the hand,

like, say, *Idahoan*. The steadily possible song

bequeaths us its mutating rooms. Its dawns. Its fizz

of micro-liberties might be the best we can ask

in an age of seclusion and pen. Of open-air prison.

Perhaps the most urgent maturity is the mortal

as mystic, a rotating someone noting the noon

of removal of difference between public and private—

that rabid hat trick of autocrat-tyranny.

Maybe the *it* we most need is one weathered hand,

scrounging its purse for an Earth certificate,

scoping the moon as it swirls a queued Orangina.

VI.

The living water flows in, but it is not channeled to where it is needed.
—Mary Midgley

The square waves of ocean
seem to suggest we should

let our innermost dwellers shift
till there's nobody left. That we

forget the self that forgets. Then what
is *there?* Attention's own dignity

sown through the senses—the body
breast-stroking outside its limbs, such that

even as whiteness lays its teeth's gel strips
across America, and while being moneyed

births the latest ethnicity—
and despite the heavy buoyance

of this message—some tranquil couplet
knows to flipper its way in.

VII.

That nervous White Man, with his heart in his mouth and his finger on his trigger, was among the most dangerous things in the jungle.
—Mary Midgley

The laws of physics being time-symmetric,

there's only ever been a single tense:

the imperfect present—its spirit-script

ripped and fusty. Tough to lay flat. The laws

of physics do not distinguish time flowing

forward from time flowing back. I guess

we've only ever known the world's glum scrim:

its Covids. Its gods' dog breath, its gated

burlesques. Each *now,* we must witness the land

scalper. The wealth supremacist. With these,

the full-on practiced refusal of whiteness to move

the wire spun round the wounds it's incurred.

   Laws of trauma lurch toward *metamorphosis:*

   what the sonnet psychs the whiteness into.

VIII.

I know when it begins to stink, you've got to do something.
                    —Mary Midgley

Fourteen	*We*	*Because*
Words,	*must*	*the*
14 or	*secure*	*beauty*
14/88	*the*	*of*
refers	*existence*	*the*
to	*of*	*White*
these	*our*	*Aryan*
14-word	*people*	*Woman*
slogans	*and*	*must*
penned	*a*	*not*
by white	*future*	*perish*
supremacist	*for*	*from*
David	*white*	*the*
Lane:	*children.*	*earth.*

IX.

You have to go round, making suitable noises.
            —Mary Midgley

    Because the white speaks the white
        Secure the white future   Because the white *For*
          Because the white *Because*

        Not the earth   because white perish Earth
Perish beauty the woman Earth   speaks the *White Must*
      because white speaks   Because White speaks *Perish*

Because White Existence Earth speaks *perish*
          Because White
    speaks white
                Because the white *Because*

~~~

Speak because Earth because woman
Because speak of the *from* of beauty

Speak of *because the not perish*
Speak from the *of* of the earth

X.

Man fears his own guilt, and insists on fixing it on something evidently alien and external.
—Mary Midgley

My junk mail comes to *Duane Raptoral*.
This makes it easy to take the other in myself
for someone else. To send what's in my skin
hate mail: gun brochures. Leaflets touting
concrete floors. I call the other *someone else's*
buzzard. My junk mail comes addressed to *Duane*
Raptoral. Since I can't trust my appetites I'll blame
the barn owl. Dub my Duane*ish* self a NASCAR driver.
Nights, I hate the dread that skids inside my smell.
I half can't bear the veer of my own tongue. I can
not seem to buck my soul's disorder. I split to live:
Mr. Raptoral, it's why I mail you gunk that ails me.
Have I stated how you're driving ourselves mad?
Sir D, you make me call the *other* someone else's me.

XI.

None of us can study anything properly unless we do it with our whole being.
—Mary Midgley

Because I can't unsee this now that someone
said the black space in Idaho's highway sign
looks like the profile of a sad Nixon. Because:
beak-nose. Because vowels roll in the jaw-bowl.
Because Frank Langella who'd played him said
Why shouldn't he be human? Sympathetic,
touching—along with the rest: vicious, cruel;
a liar, a crook? Because when Nixon started
his term, I was eight and living in Nampa, Idaho.
Because the black space is the state of Montana.
Because *Rattlesnake National Recreational Area*
battens his eyebrow. Because Idaho lights up his
profile. Because tapes. Because -gates. Because
frankly, Langella's own nose seemed to evolve.

XII.

> *I am more interested for the moment in the philosophic use of the Beast Within.*
> —Mary Midgley

*It took a long time to figure how to walk
the line,* Langella said. *I didn't want to
do an impression. I wanted an* evocation.
I wanted an essence. Then there's the matter
of Nixon's mien as state of Montana:
statesman afraid to be pinioned as fraud—
smile-scowl bruxing a path toward Bozeman,
Idaho gripped in its loft of mountains.
It's as if there's some actor-sun hyping
the archway to Nixon's mind, its forests
and caverns—the route number *8* evoking
where ear should be, its auricle-sum:
  the unabridged number of years
  to which Richard thought he was heir.

XIII.

Darwin's 'struggle for existence' can be described just as well as a mutual dependence.
—Mary Midgley

My brother fell out of the sky near Reno

and now has fierce double vision. He can sense

as each self overlaps with her inner daimonion.

He sees wakeful brains sporting twinned souls,

spots a Diane in each Duane. His probity scans

every couplet as half an octuple. It may be

some fine form of shrewdness, this shadowed

acuity, turning each *I* into towns of two people.

Their joint task: to double the number of words

meaning *we*. So, let's have this *Let's* phrase be

an example of *always inclusive.* Let's peg another

The Loyal We of the People. Let us eat five alarm chili

  on olive loaf. Let's swig and think too—how|when|whither

  feed 98 mouths of the quenchless oppressor.

XIV.

I think I must finish my toast and soup.
　　　　　　　　—Mary Midgley

When it heard the place was about to turn

minority white, the ruling class freaked.

Stripped the nation-state for its parts—

to flip every field to the oligarchs. Each tick

of whiteness sees everyday dollars beam

a Porsche to the topmost percentile. Meantime

some ingénue word gets punctured anew.

Scarcity's fact: the meanest divide is the rift

between truth and untruth, which more or less

means the primordial mouth at the birth

of the broth of language is stammering *Shit,*

you've got to be kidding me. Saying *Quick:*

tie a knapsack's vines round your middle finger

in case it needs to jet upwards in a super big hurry.

XV.

Even the dancing bee adapts to the state of her digestion.
—Mary Midgley

I'm running late for a party at Fabia's.
Mostly because of the rain. Because sometimes
language fails to deliver on anything. If only
my strain of infinity knew how to manage
a crowd. If only some phrases uncurled toting
little red frogs. If only the heart's tacit baroque.
If mainstay fragility. If fêting a labor of moles. If
never the digital oligarchs. If inner *melee* inked
its malaise. If not for the effing squirrels. If only
ripping the walls from this vowel crack house. As if
the page is always staging this putsch. As if Alamo.
As if I must beg an abbot to let me go. If hoarded
   aortae aligned to enter the commons. Be by
     in my coupe. See you in a duplet. There in a cupola.

XVI.

Feelings, to be effective, must take place as thoughts, and thoughts, to be effective, must be powered by suitable feelings.
—Mary Midgley

People are trapped by structures that lure them
to cruelty. Therefore, I build you these lines

of plucked tones, these groomed rumble strips—
this sonnet: a loaner town square with an ear

for a tune, an eye for the moves of the American
kestrel. The state keeps its head in place

wedding bodies to debt. Verifiable fact
droops on the lip of extinction. So, this town

will enact a conscious recoupling of feeling
with thought through sentence pair-bonding.

Therefore, these mansions of makeshift planks
might soothe a few anatomies of brute existence.

Squat and keen: To stitch and tune the suffering
of meaning—take and eat. This is our flesh.

XVII.

Every age has its pet contradictions.
            —Mary Midgley

Brambled into the planet's absurdities:
ads' airraids. Survival silos. A bursitis

of oligarchs—American tsars braying
post-primacy arias. Scrambled within

the world's absurdities: weird phrases,
like *turnt* and *worth your follow.* The hand-

bra. Thirty million acres of arable U.S. land
held by foreign investors. The disinvention

of empathy. That cruelty is coin of pleasure.
That *Soul* is a Kia. That *Ikea* is even a word.

That absurdity knows to beer its own university.
That absurdity drubs its outré sutras.

That *whites above all.* That *men above Earth.*
That I cannot drive a stick to eternity's yurt.

XVIII.

You feel akin to the whole thing.
—Mary Midgley

The sonnet's a prison I lock myself in
so I can find new ways to break free.
You know that endurance artist/
illusionist who locked himself inside
that plexiglass box for 44 days? Even
a webcam watch didn't bar theories of
David Blaine holograms, his hooligan
stunt-doubles. Oh, the self is as much
a drop as it is a daze of rangy acreage:
this vaporish series of dits and dahs,
a heart thumping six feet away from itself.
So why do I finally want to admit I feel
like this slutty glut of a super-unity—dangling
over the Thames in a dweeb's rectangle?

XIX.

The beast within us gives us partial order.
—Mary Midgley

Number 14 rings with a keen single-mindedness:
Knows to lean into life's code of intensities, says
Tru Numerology—14's pair of sevens encrypted
in pieces by Bach. Counting from one to 14
can take 13 short breaths. This intensifies sex.
Simply playing cantatas means we might pause
a shared numbness. Fourteen finds it often struggles
with too many interests, i.e., how a woodlouse
scissors its 14 legs in 2 rivers of 7. How time thinks
it's ripe to flick out a line to the 5th Dimension.
14 prefers that its flights of genuity further a goal:
to unshine brutality's boot heel. To remind how
money's a thing as made up as inches. How to
chip out a self from one's own number-anguish.

XX.

Life-long opponents can end up as almost undistinguishable from each other.
—Mary Midgley

Swimming these song laps frees the mind's ear.

Besides, it increases my wrist flexors' range

to continue to bail on my own false self.

I apprize my autonomies while at the same time

turning an eye toward America's run at self-rule.

This country's a murk I must cruise. In its

waters: this fantasy wall of *us's* and *thems*.

No such thing as an earlier innocence.

Never a leader eloped with the people. So,

when it's time to swim-sing, I make myself

sizeless in every direction, forging the open turn,

where the swimmer kisses the wall with two hands,

tucks her thighs in, and then—with this push-off—

totally butterflies into the opposite side of the pool.

XXI.

Hubris calls for nemesis, and in one form or another it's going to get it, not as a punishment from outside but as the completion of a pattern already started.

—Mary Midgley

The last liberal president in recent*ish*

history was—wait for it—because it wasn't

Obama or William Clinton. Nor was he Lyndon

B. Johnson. Or James Earl Carter. While JFK

makes for decent conjecture, he's not it either.

Neither is Harry S. Truman, whose middle initial

served as two granddads' placeholder: *Shippe*

and *Solomon.* Modern history's most liberal

president: Dick Millhouse Nixon. Why? He openly

feared people's movements. *I am sure,* he'd said

to his aides, *they're coming to get us. They're going to*

break through the barriers…BTW Nixon's *I* was his

me. By *they,* he meant *we.* By *us,* he meant *them.*

And this be the verse—my brothers, my sisters.

[The Floating Sonnet, Unnumbered]

We are not usually in lifeboats.
　　　—Mary Midgley

The self puts itself between *I* and the other:

This leads each to repeat cruelties.

There is no other; therefore, there's no *I*.

The merge of subject-object is Nirvana's mother.

There is no *this|that;* therefore, there's no *either*.

The self recreates things other than they are:

There is no *I*, and thus I lung inside my brother.

The merge of subject-object is Nirvana's daughter.

If it isn't one thing, it's the thing's father.

The *I* arcs its foot between sockeye and river.

There is no other; therefore, there's no *I*.

There and *Not-there* swap hymns with each other.

　First and last names simply make for good cover.

　　　Our *we* flings its signature in untraceable air~~

About the Author

Diane Raptosh's collection *American Amnesiac* (Etruscan Press), was longlisted for the 2013 National Book Award in poetry. The recipient of three fellowships in literature from the Idaho Commission on the Arts, she served as the Boise Poet Laureate (2013) as well as the Idaho Writer-in-Residence (2013–2016). In 2018 she won the Idaho Governor's Arts Award in Excellence. She teaches literature and creative writing and co-directs the program in Criminal Justice/Prison Studies at the College of Idaho. Her seventh collection, *Run: A Verse-History of Victoria Woodhull,* was published by Etruscan Press in 2021 as part of the multi-author volume, *Trio*.

dianeraptosh.com

www.ingramcontent.com/pod-product-compliance
Lightning Source LLC
Chambersburg PA
CBHW071642090426

42738CB00013B/3191